PRINTER'S ABECEDARIUM

PRINTER'S
ABECEDARIUM

by
JOHN O. C. McCRILLIS

Edited by Susan C. McCrillis

David R. Godine, Publisher
Boston

David R. Godine Publisher
Boston, Massachusetts

Copyright © 1974 by David R. Godine, Publisher
ISBN 0-87923-107-6
LCC 74-81517

FOREWORD: Instruction with delight, that exemplary eighteenth century ap⁄proach to education, helped inspire count⁄less graphic toys and games for learning. Among the most successful and enduring of these didactic amusements was the alphabet book. In Colonial America, the form emerged in the New England Primer and introduced the alphabet's A to young readers along with original sin. 'In Adam's fall we sinnéd all.' Later editions softened this grim Biblical lesson to that pleasant ultimate in alphabetical platitudes: 'A is for Apple.'

¶Ever more subtle variations in the al⁄phabet book form followed in the nine⁄teenth century. Many French abecedaires are beautifully lithographed, and even gild⁄ed and printed on silk. An accordion for⁄mat in two charming English alphabets by Cruikshank and Gordon Craig turn these small books into true ABC pano⁄ramas. Sharply satirical alphabets by French artists such as Daumier and Victor Adam were popular in the caricature journal Charivari. Verbal obsession with alphabet⁄ical alliteration also led to that great tongue⁄twisting classic, Peter Piper's Practical Principals of Plain and Perfect Pronuncia⁄tion, published in England in 1813.

⊂In our own time the alphabet book con⁄
tinues to flourish in great variety. Edward
Gorey, in his <u>Gashlycrumb Tinies</u>, ex⁄
tends and slightly warps the ABC tradi⁄
tion with twenty⁄six little descendants of
Kate Greenaway meeting untimely ends,
from Amy who fell down the stairs to
Zillah who drank too much gin. Maurice
Sendak has a lighter touch with his <u>Alli⁄</u>
<u>gators All Around</u>, where large lovely
lizards are seen Doing Dishes, Getting
Giggles, or Wearing Wigs. Even porno⁄
graphy has its alphabetical day in the
highly sophisticated ABC creation of
Jules Pascin.

⊂The durable appeal of alphabet books
has also resulted in a great many properly
sober A to Z correlations for almost every
area of learning from Authors to Zoolo⁄
gy. It is highly appropriate that the history
of the art of printing should also have
its alphabet book. John McCrillis, in his
<u>Printer's Abecedarium</u>, has pursued the
idea to create his own alphabetical Pan⁄
theon of great printers.

⊂The McCrillis Abecedarium also gives
homage to the twenty⁄six letters of the
alphabet with the utmost finesse of pres⁄
entation and historical aptness. Each Goth⁄
ic letter has been freely adapted from the

illuminated initials found in the Yale Li⁄
brary copy of the <u>Catholicon</u>, thought to
have been printed by Gutenberg at Mainz
in 1460. The resulting McCrillis design is
a triumphal exercise in the revival of letter
forms. In significant addition to its abbre⁄
viated dictionary of printers from Aldus
to Zainer, the McCrillis Abecedarium
gives us a latter⁄day calligraphic model
book, masterfully printed and worthy of
its fine fifteenth⁄century inspiration.

Dale Roylance, Curator
Arts of the Book Room
Yale University Library

ALDUS MANUTIUS, 1450/1515, a Renaissance Venetian printer and type designer, was noted for his innovative approach to typography. He eschewed gothic type, using greek and roman, and later inventing italic types.

⁋The first of his successful type faces was that of the De Aetna, written by Pietro Bembo, published in 1495, and considered by some to be the first mod/ern book in terms of typographic style. The roots of the font were calligraphic, but there was no comparison among other contemporary types.

⁋This and subsequent styles were highly appreciated by French printers, notably Garamond and Granjon, and the French versions were so good that they found their way back to Italy, initiating an ex/change of styles that led to the develop/ment of "old face" types.

The inventor of "modern" type faces was JOHN BASKERVILLE, 1706/1775, a wealthy Birmingham writing master and decorator of japanned tinware. Printing was an avocation with Basker/ville; his was the first truly private press. ⁋Dissatisfied with existing types, he spent two years designing his own; they were lighter in character and had pointed serifs rather than the rounded or club/shaped ones characteristic of old/style faces. Recognizing the inadequacies of the available printers' inks, he manufactured his own, even boiling the oil and burning the lampblack himself. Laid paper did not suit him, so he invented a technique to manufacture wove paper/the first ever. Newly/printed sheets were pressed be/tween hot copper plates to dry and set the ink, giving the paper a smooth and pol/ished finish.

⁋These innovations required time and ex/pense; it took Baskerville seven years to produce his first book. Ornaments were used sparingly and the design was elegant and chaste. Because of his perfection, and because he didn't begin printing until he was forty/four years old, he published only about 56 books in his career, his most ambitious work being the folio Bible, completed in 1763.

WILLIAM CAXTON, born in England about 1422, began his career as an apprentice to a wealthy wool merchant. After 1441 he established his own business in Bruges and prospered in the double role of merchant and diplomat.

⚏Caxton translated into English the popular French Recueil des Histoires de Troye and became so interested in the project that he went to Cologne to learn the new art of printing so that he might publish his translation. Returning to Bruges, he and Colard Mansion, a clever calligrapher, founded a press there.

⚏In 1476 Caxton moved to Westminster, taking some type and equipment with him. There he established England's first press. His first dated book was issued a year later, and was entitled The Dictes or Sayengis of the Philosophres. Chaucer's Canterbury Tales followed. These books were illustrated and intended for popular rather than scholarly use. By the time of his death in 1491, Caxton had printed and published nearly a hundred titles.

STEPHEN DAYE, c. 1594/1668, was born in London and was a locksmith by trade. He ventured forth with the Reverend Jose Glover in 1638 to set up a printing press in the English colonies of North America. Glover died at sea and Daye was left to do the job himself. The equipment for the venture consisted of a printing press and type, three pressmen and a printer. It was set up in Cambridge, Massachusetts in the autumn of 1638 under the auspices of the president of Harvard College.

⁋The first issue from the press was the Freeman's Oath in January, 1639. Next came an Almanack by William Pierce the same year. In the following year the book known as the Bay Psalm Book appeared. ⁋Other extant issues from the Stephen Daye press are another Almanack, a list of Theses at the Harvard Commencement and a primer of the Indian language by John Eliot which was printed by Samuel Green and Marmaduke Johnson and completed in 1663.

The ENSCHEDÉ foundry and print/ ing office in Haarlem, Netherlands, was founded in 1703 and is flourishing today, still with an Enschedé in charge. It pos/ sesses probably the best private collection of ancient types in the world, some dating from the fifteenth century.

⁋In the firm's early history Isaac and Jo/ hannes Enschedé bought up other found/ ries or portions thereof, resulting in their remarkable collection. These acquisitions included types by Rudolph Wetstein, his father, G. Wetstein, and also some fonts cut by Christoffel Van Dyck. The Enschedé printing office was among the first to print polyphonic music and even printed music for Leopold Mozart.

⁋In more recent times Jan Van Krimpen added luster to the already substantial glow of the foundry with his restrained and elegant <u>Lutetia</u>, <u>Romanée</u>, <u>Romulus</u>, and <u>Spectrum</u> typefaces.

⁋Van Krimpen's colleague and successor, Sem L. Hartz, continues contributing to and enhancing the house with his distin/ guished designing and printing. That En/ schedé still designs and prints stamps and currency for many nations is testament that its quality, now a tradition for nearly 275 years, remains undiminished.

PIERRE SIMON FOURNIER (le jeune), 1712/1768, was a member of a family noted for its contributions to the development of printing. His father was the manager of the Le Bé foundry for thirty years, and his brother, Fournier l'aîné, was an engraver and typefounder. Fournier l'aîné purchased the Le Bé foundry with its collection of ancient types upon his father's death in 1730. Since Fournier le jeune was educated in art, he was well prepared to continue this tradition by cutting wood blocks, engraving punches and producing several fonts of type and type "flowers". He also formulated a point system (subsequently modified) for measuring type sizes, and designed such outstanding music type that he was appointed supernumerary printer of music for Louis XV. An italic type of his design was fine and regular and became immediately popular. Entirely the work of his own hands, his foundry's yield was an achievement unique in printing history. Fournier le jeune also wrote and published the Manuel Typographique, the first book in French on type and typefounding, an excellent source of information.

JOHANN GUTENBERG, c. 1397/1468, was born in Mainz and was a goldsmith by trade. His greatest achievement was not the invention of printing per se, which had been done in China for centuries, but ra/ ther in the perfection of the type mould, allowing large quantities of identical and individual letters to be cast, each aligning with the other, each independent and re/ usable. He perfected the principle of mov/ able type. Gutenberg's task was long and difficult. He borrowed money from Jo/ hann Fust, who became his partner in the production of the first book printed from movable type, his 42/line Bible. This mon/ ument to taste, faith and craftsmanship es/ tablished a standard which has never been subsequently equalled.

⟨Gutenberg was unable to repay the loans before the books were sold and Fust fore/ closed. After this time he is believed to have assisted in production of a 36/line Bible and in the printing of a <u>Catholicon</u> by Johannes Balbus in 1460. This encyclo/ pedic dictionary of the Latin language was the first secular book ever to be printed.

⟨The decorative initials in this Abeceda/ rium were modeled after the hand/painted initials in the <u>Catholicon</u> at the Beinecke Library, Yale University.

JOHANN HEYNLIN, born in the Duchy of Baden, by 1470 had been prior and rector of the Sorbonne in Paris. He was a booklover and was acquainted with printers in Mainz. He interested Fichet, professor of belles/lettres and rhetoric at the Sorbonne, in a plan to import print/ers to Paris so that learned works could be more correctly done than by hand copy/ists of the time. Three printers were sent for, Freiburger, an educated man and friend of Heynlin's, and two other workmen, Ul/rich Gering and Martin Kranz. Thus the first printing house in France was estab/lished. Before printing anything, the three imported craftsmen were obliged to manu/facture the tools of their trade, to set up a press, to fit up their workroom and to cut their type. Since Heynlin, who was near/sighted, was to correct proof, a large roman character was selected in preference to a Gothic manuscript letter, which was generally used in France at that time.

¶ By 1477 Freiburger and Kranz had re/turned to Germany, and Fichet had gone to Italy. Heynlin was no longer taking an active part. Ulrich Gering has been con/sidered the patriarch of Parisian typogra/phy, and he prospered, but it was Heynlin who was responsible for his beginning.

The IMPRIMERIE ROYALE du Lou-vre, brainchild of Cardinal Richelieu, was installed on November 17, 1640. Richelieu was intrigued by contemporary Dutch printing, and particularly by a special ink perfected in the Netherlands, so he re-quested at least four Dutch compositors and four pressmen, including one who knew the ink formula, to come to France and operate the establishment. For a legi-ble roman, Richelieu also called upon the Jannon foundry at Sedan to produce the type first used at the Imprimerie.

¶ In 1692 Philippe Grandjean was com-missioned by Louis XIV to design a new typeface for the exclusive use of the royal printing house. This font, the romain du roi, had thin, horizontal serifs, an advance-ment toward a 'modern' typeface, derived more from engraving than from calligra-phy. To distinguish it as a royal font, the lower case 'l' was given a little projection on the left of the shank, a practice which was used for all fonts cut for the Imprimerie Royale thereafter.

¶ Grandjean was succeeded by Alexandre, then by Louis Luce, both royal type cut-ters. Luce's type ornaments were particu-larly beautiful, harmonizing well with his types. Luce was succeeded by Fagnon, the last of the royal type cutters.

NICOLAUS JENSON, c. 1420/1480, was a Frenchman who early in his career became mint-master at Tours. About 1458 he apparently was sent to Mainz by King Charles VII to bring back information on the new art of printing. But the king died in 1461 and it is not known if Jenson ever returned to France.

⁋Jenson next appeared in Venice where he established the second Venetian press, having been preceded by Johannes and Wendelin da Spira. Johannes printed his first book in 1469 in a new roman type based on the Italian humanistic hand. Although he received five years' protection for his roman type he died a year later, and the restriction was lifted. Jenson, who may have designed da Spira's type in the first place, perfected his own roman in the same year da Spira died. Jenson's type used in his <u>Eusebius</u> is regarded by many as having the most admirable qualities in its design as a reading text. It was closely copied by modern master typographers such as Emery Walker, T. J. Cobden Sanderson and Bruce Rogers.

⁋Jenson continued to design roman, gothic and greek types of particular distinction until his death in Rome in 1480.

ANTON KOBERGER of Nuremberg, c. 1445/1513, was a highly successful print/er, publisher and bookseller. He estab/lished a printing plant with twenty/four presses and a staff of a hundred craftsmen. He built a book trade which extended from the surrounding German cities to Paris, Milan, Bologna, Florence, Lyons, Venice, and Krakow.

⁋ Koberger's volumes were large and am/bitious, surpassing all others published in Nuremberg. His two greatest works were the Schatzbehalter, a religious treatise, and the Nuremberg Chronicle, both illustra/ted by Dürer's teacher, Michael Wolge/mut. There are ninety/four full/page wood/cuts in the Schatzbehalter, mostly scenes from the scriptures. In the Nuremberg Chronicle there are over eighteen hun/dred woodcut illustrations, and it was pub/lished in both Latin and German editions. Koberger issued more than two hundred titles, most of them large folios, including fifteen Bibles. In 1480 he distributed an ad/vertisement for a theological work stat/ing it had been printed in the same type as the book. If anyone wished to buy the volume, he could do so from his agent at the inn. Thus Koberger very early made use of the advertising circular.

GUILLAUME LE BÉ I, 1525/1598, born at Troyes, was a pupil of Garamond and Estienne. He went, as they did, to Rome and Venice to perfect his work as a type/founder and engraver. At the age of twen/ty/one he cut his first Hebrew types, and was the first engraver of oriental types in the world.

⁋ Le Bé and his son, Guillaume Le Bé II, collected and preserved many matrices of characters in use since the beginning of printing. Le Bé I also engraved music for Leroy and Ballard, the earliest Parisian music printers.

⁋ In 1561 Le Bé bought most of the punch/es and matrices of Garamond's types and almost all of the material from his foundry.

⁋ Jean Claude Fournier directed the Le Bé foundry for twenty/five years. In 1730 his son, Fournier l'aîné, bought the found/ry with all its ancient punches, strikes and matrices.

MAINZ, at the confluence of the Rhine and Main rivers, was the first great center for European printing. Here the printed book became the ambitious rival of the manuscript.

⸿ Johann Gutenberg, largely responsible for the development of the city's new trade, began and ended his life there. Continuing Gutenberg's achievement, Johann Fust and Peter Schoeffer printed their Psalter, the first book to bear a printed date, a printer's device and a colophon.

⸿ Printers from Mainz went out to every important city in Europe. Nicolaus Jenson traveled from Paris to Mainz to study the new art of printing, then journeyed to Venice to pursue the trade. Freiburger, Ulrich Gering and Martin Kranz left the city to establish the first printing office in Paris. Mainz goldsmith Johannes da Spira and his brother Wendelin became the first Venetian printers. Conrad Sweynheym also brought his printing expertise to Italy.

⸿ So the influence of many fifteenth-century printers traced its origin to the city of Mainz.

GEORGE NICOL, bookseller to King George III, was passionately interested in improving the typography of his time. To this end he hired the great punchcutter, William Martin, who had learned his trade in Baskerville's foundry, to cut new types after the style of Didot and Bodoni.

¶ Nicol was a member of a coterie that enjoyed typographical experiments and existed for the purpose of combining the trades of printing, typefounding, engraving and paper-making to create typography of superior quality. Included in this group were John and Josiah Boydell, patrons of fine printing, George and W. Nicol, booksellers, Thomas and John Bewick, wood engravers, and William Bulmer, printer. To indulge their tastes, they established a shop, called it the W. Bulmer and Co. Shakspeare Press, and printed such typographic masterpieces as the 'Boydell Shakspeare,' 1792-1802, the Milton of 1794-97, and Poems by Goldsmith and Parnell, 1795.

The OXFORD PRESS, now known as the Oxford University Press, was founded in 1585 and has been in continous operation ever since. It has been collecting type since 1629, when Sir Henry Savile gave the press some fine Greek fonts. Between 1667 and 1672 Dr. John Fell, later bishop of Oxford, presented the press with some remarkable specimens imported from Holland. Neglected for many years, these 'Fell' types regained popularity in the middle of the nineteenth century and are now one of the great prides of the press.

¶ Dr. Fell helped establish both the Wolvercote paper mill, which later became the property of the press, and also a foundry. His types, still cast and used in the production of Oxford books today, are responsible in large part for the press's reputation for distinguished printing. Perhaps the best recent example of fine printing is the Oxford Lectern Bible by Bruce Rogers and John Johnson. Produced in 1935, it was set in Rogers's Centaur type, modified to fit the project, and is a superb example of the attention to production quality typical of Oxford books.

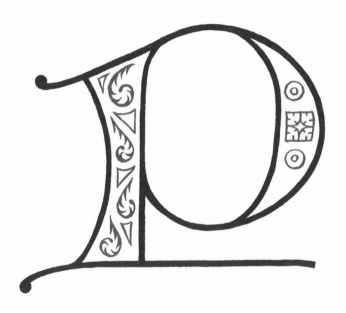

The Officina PLANTINIANA is lo⁄
cated in Antwerp. To quote D. B. Updike,
it is 'more a palace than a printing house⁄
has long been, and still is, one of the sights
of Europe. It is probably the most beautiful
building dedicated to the uses of printing.'
❡ In 1555 Christopher Plantin, a French⁄
man, founded the house and after his death
in 1589, it was managed by Johan More⁄
tus I, Plantin's son⁄in⁄law. Thus the press
was called the Plantin⁄Moretus Office.
❡ In 1875 it was ceded to the city by Ed⁄
ouard Moretus, the last proprietor. The
presses, type, and materials of Plantin,
Moretus, and their successors, plus the
account books and correspondence, have all
been preserved. Along with the remarkable
typographic collection, there are also orig⁄
inal plates, wood blocks, ornaments, bind⁄
ing tools and designs commissioned for
the press by such artists as Rubens.
❡ Entire rooms are open for public in⁄
spection: the typecutter's workshop, the
foundry, the pressroom and the proof⁄
room. These rooms, remarkable for the
fidelity of their detail, succeed in giving
a uniquely accurate view of an early print⁄
ing office.

QUEEN ELIZABETH'S Prayer Book was the common name for <u>A Book of Christian Prayers</u>, printed by John Day in 1569.

⁋D. B. Updike, in his <u>Printing Types</u>, Harvard University Press, 1937, doesn't think much of its typography ⁄ 'a rough, tasteless black⁄letter volume, clumsily modelled on French <u>Horae</u>, but which had great popularity'.

⁋But John Day was a London printer who distinguished himself with his early sixteenth century English typography. His <u>Ælfredi Regis Res Gestæ</u>, printed in 1574, shows a very fine roman and italic type, superior to almost any other type founding of the period.

ERHARD RATDOLT, 1442/1528, a printer and type⁄cutter from Augsburg, came to Venice in 1476 and embarked on a publishing career which was to produce among the more distinguished titles of the fifteenth century. His books became fa⁄mous for their extremely fine borders, glorious initial letters, fine presswork, in⁄corporation of color and decorative title pages. In his <u>Calendarium</u> of Regiomon⁄tanus, 1476, he was the first printer to pre⁄sent a 'modern' title page including the book's title, printer and date of issue.

¶ Ratdolt was also the first to issue a specimen sheet. Appearing in 1486, it ex⁄hibited three fonts of good quality; ten sizes of gothic letter, three sizes of roman and a specimen of Greek.

¶ The type chosen for this book, Inku⁄nabula, is based on a font of Ratdolt's de⁄sign. Introduced in 1911 by the Societa Augusta of Turin, it is a testament to the lasting appeal of Ratdolt's typographic achievements.

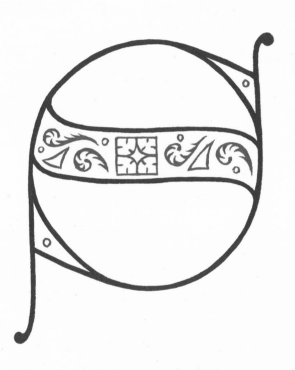

PETER SCHOEFFER, c. 1425/1502/3, came from Gernsheim, Germany. He was employed by Gutenberg during the preparation of the Gutenberg Bible, but when Gutenberg became heavily indebted to Johann Fust, his financial backer, Fust foreclosed, ousted Gutenberg and made Peter Schoeffer his partner, forming a very successful business.

¶ In 1457 Fust and Schoeffer finished their great Psalter, the first book with a colophon carrying the name of the printer and date of publication. They were also the first to use a printer's mark, a symbol previously used only by tradesmen. Their device showed a double shield hung from a branch.

¶ The Psalter was the first book to print elaborate colored initials; red and blue and sometimes gray. Before this innovation initials were individually hand-colored by a rubricator.

¶ Besides the Psalter two other magnificent books were printed by Fust and Schoeffer. They are a Bible printed in 1462 and a Cicero in 1465.

¶ Peter Schoeffer, who became the son-in-law of Johann Fust, continued to print, publish and sell books, broadsheets and pamphlets until his death.

GEOFFROY TORY, 1480/1533, was a Latin and Greek scholar, poet, translator, lecturer and critic. More important for the history of printing, he was also an artist, cal/ ligrapher, type designer, engraver, printer, and publisher.

⸿A Frenchman, Tory traveled to Italy and was greatly influenced by the typo/ graphy of the southern Italian Renais/ sance. When he returned he brought with him a refined taste largely responsible for the remarkable beauty and delicacy of French printing in the sixteenth century. His Book of Hours, printed in 1525 by Simon de Colines, is a prime example of this new typographic trend. Its beautiful floral borders and decorations balance in perfect harmony with the roman type. Tory also designed initial letters, head/ pieces, and typographic flowers of partic/ ular charm and elegance.

⸿His Champfleury, issued in 1529, in/ cluded a treatise on roman capital letters and compared their proportions to those of the human body. This book, a typo/ graphic classic of high order, won for him the distinction of being named imprimeur du roi.

JOHANN FREDERIC UNGER, 1750/1804, was a printer and typefounder in Berlin. Like his contemporaries Firmin Didot and Giambattista Bodoni, Unger was interested in developing a lightness in typography. His types were mostly fraktur and schwabacher letter forms, but he did cut some roman types as well.

¶ About 1791 Unger issued Schriftproben der Didotschen und Gewöhnlichen Let͵ tern, containing types of his own design. The light strokes and thin serifs of his italics did not work well at all, but some of the Ordinaire Deutsch Lettern, both fraktur and schwabacher, were fine and robust.

¶ Unger's Wilhelm Meister, published in 1795, shows the success in achieving the lightness of typography that he had pro͵ moted in his specimen book.

VENICE was the leading commercial city in Europe of the fifteenth century. With its wealth and cosmopolitan flavor, it is no wonder that it attracted printers with their newly acquired skills. Many of the early Venetian printers who learned their trade in Mainz and came directly to Venice included Johann and Wendelin da Spira, the first printers to arrive in 1469, Nicolaus Jenson in 1470, and Erhard Ratdolt, who began printing in 1476. By 1471 there were five printers in Venice; by 1472 there were twelve.

¶ Probably the greatest printer-scholar to have a publishing office in Venice was Aldus Manutius. His Poliphilus, 1499, was a classic of Renaissance book illustration and typography. He was also responsible for the invention of the italic letter, cut by Francesco Griffo in 1501 and based on a cursive version of the humanistic hand.

¶ Lucantonio Giunta printed illustrated editions, including his Malermi Bible, and Giacomo Giunta, from the same family, printed his Triompho di Fortuna, 1527, in Venice, although the family branches were in both Venice and Florence.

WYNKYN de WORDE, d. 1534?, an Alsatian, apparently came to England with William Caxton in 1476 and became his foreman. He took over the printing office in 1491, when Caxton died, and in his long career turned out close to 800 editions. Also a typefounder, he improved on the English types of his time, making them more like the French and Italian types of the period.

¶ De Worde was not an innovative printer; he seemed content to do reprints of Caxton's editions or those of other printers. His most original work was <u>All the Proprytees of Thynges</u> by Bartholomeus, printed in 1495, and he issued the earliest collection of Christmas carols six years later.

¶ In 1500 de Worde moved from Caxton's old quarters to Fleet Street, the first publisher on a thoroughfare that would later become known throughout the world as the center of English publishing.

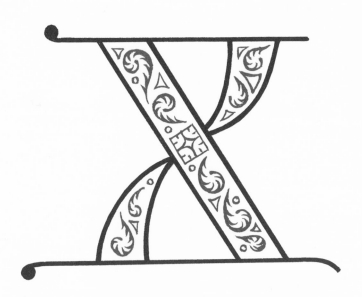

FRANCISCUS Cardinal XIMENEZ de Cisneros, 1435/1517, was a Spanish prel/ate and statesman, Confessor to Queen Isabella, inquisitor general of Castile and Leon, Archbishop of Toledo, founder of the University of Alcalá, and patron of the art of printing.

⁊ Ximenez took financial responsibility for one of the great masterpieces of Span/ish typography, namely, the Compluten/sian Bible, printed by Guillen de Brocar between 1514/1517. It was the first of the great Polyglots and was printed in He/brew, Chaldee, Greek, and Latin and was in six folio volumes. The title page of the first volume showed the arms of Cisneros surmounted by a cardinal's hat. The Greek types used in the New Testament were famous because they preserved the charac/ter of older Greek manuscripts, based on an early book/hand.

⁊ The whole undertaking of the Com/plutensian Bible, started in 1502, with the printing beginning in 1514. Although the printing was finished in 1517, the Bible was not published until 1522, five years after the cardinal's death. It cost Ximenez 50,000 gold ducats, equivalent to well over a million dollars.

JOACHIN YBARRA (Ibarra), 1725/
1785, remains the best/known Spanish
printer. Benjamin Franklin, who was ac/
quainted with Ybarra's work, said the Sal/
lust and the Don Quixote equalled in
quality any printing he had ever seen.

⁋ Ybarra was certainly influenced by the
work of Bodoni and possibly by that of
Didot and Baskerville. While printer to
the Spanish Court, his masterpiece was a
Spanish and Latin edition of the Sallust,
Cayo Salustio Crispo en Espanol, printed
in 1772. Other great books printed by him
were the Royal Academy edition of Don
Quixote, a Mozarabic Breviary, Mariana's
Historia de España, and Antonio's Biblio/
theca Hispana, Vetus et Nova.

⁋ Ybarra's sumptuous editions were dis/
tinguished by their beautiful engravings,
choice types, their typographic accuracy
and their fine presswork.

GUNTHER ZAINER, fl. 1468/1478, a scribe and illuminator, learned the print/ing trade from Johann Mentelin in the town of Strasbourg and then set up his shop in Augsburg. He wanted to use wood/cut illustrations in his books but an early example of the power of the printers' unions blocked his endeavors. They threatened suit unless he agreed to have the wood/cuts made by members of the woodcutters' guild.

⁋ Zainer agreed, and his first two illustrat/ed books were printed in 1471 and 1472. His most popular book was <u>Spiegel des menschlichen Lebens</u>, printed about 1476. This has a perfect blending of gothic type, woodcut illustrations, and woodcut initial letters. In the same year Zainer produced one of the first printed illustrated Bibles, containing illustrations within large his/toriated initials.

⁋ Zainer died in 1478, but in his short career as a printer he produced over a hundred editions.

The AMPERSAND is a corruption of 'and per se, and'. It is also a monogram of the two letters et. Its purpose was primarily decorative since it occupied no less linear space than the latin word et.

⁋Marcus Tullius Tiro, secretary to Cicero, used a symbol representing et early in the first century B.C., but it looked like our arabic numeral 7. The earliest monogram of the latin et resembling a ligature et occurs in a seventh century manuscript of St. Maximus. This symbol occurred frequently in manuscripts from that time on, and sometimes the ligature was used within a word as well, such as &iam (etiam).

⁋It is interesting to note that the symbol resembling a figure 7 appeared in early examples of printing, especially with blackletter types. When the roman types appeared, the symbol representing the et ligature took precedence, and the Tironian symbol 7 diminished in use.

ACKNOWLEDGMENTS: I am in⁄
debted to Kenneth M. Nesheim, Asso⁄
ciate Director of the Beinecke Rare Book
and Manuscript Library at Yale Univer⁄
sity, for permission to have pages of the
Yale copy of the <u>Catholicon</u> by Johannes
Balbus photographed. This book was
printed in Mainz in 1460 and is attributed
to Johann Gutenberg.
⟨ My thanks to William K. Sacco for his
expert photography in making prints from
which letters in this book have been de⁄
signed; to Henry B. White for use of his
Inkunabula type which seems appropriate
for the text; to Gerard E. Fredette, with⁄
out whose help in pulling reproduction
proofs and valiant assistance in the type⁄
setting, this book might never have come
to light.
⟨ To my daughter, Susan, I am especially
grateful for her keen interest in the pro⁄
ject and for her able editing of the manu⁄
script. To my wife, Barbara, I am grateful
for her patience in bearing up when the
book took precedence over all household
matters.

The text of this book has been composed by hand in 18 point Inkunabula type. The two-color initials, designed by the author, are reproduced the same size as the originals. The book was designed by the author and printed on 80 lb. Mohawk Superfine softwhite. The printing has been done by The Meriden Gravure Company and the binding by Robert Burlen & Sons.